SCIENCE BUZZWORDS

Is It Heavy?

For a free color catalog describing Gareth Stevens Publishing's list of high-quality books and multimedia programs, call 1-800-542-2595 (USA) or 1-800-461-9120 (Canada). Gareth Stevens Publishing's Fax: (414) 225-0377.
See our catalog, too, on the World Wide Web: http://gsinc.com

Library of Congress Cataloging-in-Publication Data

Bryant-Mole, Karen.
    Is it heavy? / Karen Bryant-Mole.
      p. cm. — (Science buzzwords)
    Originally published: London: A & C Black (Publishers), 1995.
    Includes index.
    Summary: Suggests the right words for describing sizes and amounts, from "short" to "tall" to "deep" and "shallow."
    ISBN 0-8368-1727-3 (lib. bdg.)
    1. Vocabulary—Juvenile literature. 2. Size perception—Juvenile literature. [1. Size. 2. Vocabulary.] I. Title. II. Series.
PE1449.B793 1997
428.1—dc20   96-38738

First published in North America in 1997 by
Gareth Stevens Publishing
1555 North RiverCenter Drive, Suite 201
Milwaukee, WI 53212 USA

The author and publisher would like to thank all the children who appear in the photographs. They also wish to thank the Early Learning Centre, Swindon, for providing the equipment featured on pages 2 and 3.

Printed in the United States of America

1 2 3 4 5 6 7 8 9 01 00 99 98 97

SCIENCE BUZZWORDS

Is It Heavy?

Karen Bryant-Mole

Gareth Stevens Publishing
MILWAUKEE

short

Leila has used a few blocks
to make a **short** tower.

tall

Leila is using many blocks
to make a **tall** tower.

taller

Lou's sister is **taller** than Lou.

tallest

Lou's mom is taller than Lou and his sister.
Lou's mom is the **tallest**.

long

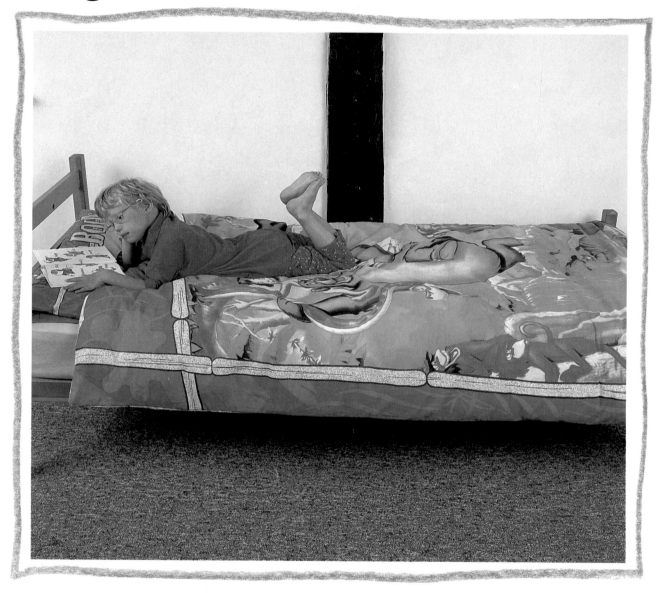

Alex is lying on a **long** bed.
There is plenty of room to stretch out.

short

Her doll's bed is **short**.
Could Alex stretch out in it?

shorter

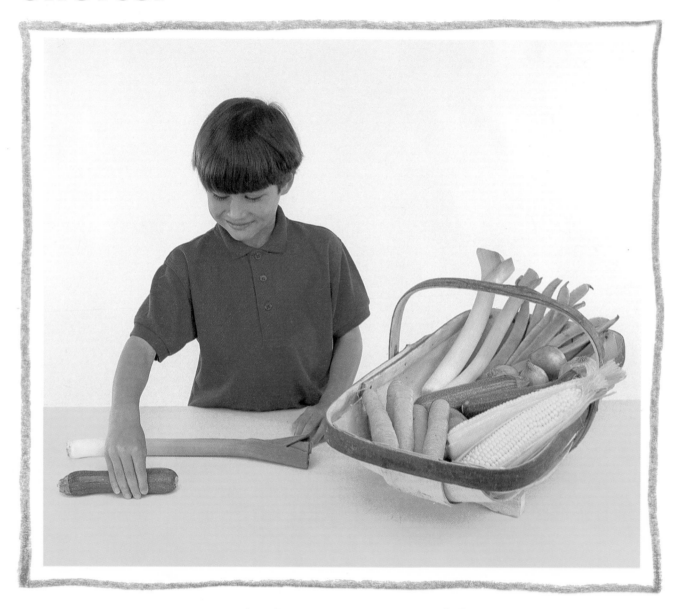

Sam has some vegetables.
The zucchini is **shorter** than the leek.

shortest

But the carrot is the **shortest**
of all three vegetables.

large

An elephant is a **large** animal.
You can sit on top of an elephant.

small

A guinea pig is **small**.
You can hold one in your arms.

thin

Charlie is eating a **thin** sandwich.
He has no trouble holding it.

thick

Leila is eating a **thick** sandwich.
Her sandwich is hard to hold!

wide

Holly opens the **wide** gate
to let the tractor through.

narrow

Emma and Leila open the **narrow**
gate and come through.

full

Lou's glass is **full** of milk.
He must be very thirsty.

empty

Lou drank all of the milk.
His glass is now **empty**.

deep

In the **deep** swimming pool, the water comes up to Sarah's chin.

shallow

In the **shallow** wading pool, the water only comes up to her ankles.

heavy

Charlie's box is full of toys.
It is too **heavy** for him to carry.

light

Sam's box of candy is easy to carry.
It is very **light**.

balanced

Emma sits on one end of the seesaw.
Leila sits on the other end.

Both ends are off the ground.
The seesaw is **balanced**.

How to Use This Book

Children's understanding of concepts is fundamentally linked to their ability to comprehend and use relevant language. This book is designed to help children understand the vocabulary associated with **measurement**.

Measurement is an important area within mathematics. Before children can begin to measure using standard units, they need to understand that objects have sizes and quantities. This book helps children develop that understanding by explaining key words connected with measurement and by encouraging children to use these words in everyday situations.

Most of the pairs of words featured on each double page are opposites, such as *full* and *empty*. Other pairs of words, such as *taller* and *tallest*, are comparative. Children can be encouraged to think about the words and to discuss whether the words are opposites or not.

Each word in this book is presented through a color photograph and a phrase, which uses the word in context. Besides explaining words basic to the understanding of measurement, the book can also be used in a number of other ways.

Children can think of objects, other than the ones in the photographs, that can be described using a particular Science Buzzword. For example, the Buzzword *wide* does not just describe gates. It can be applied to many other objects, as well. Roads, trailers, rivers, and tires can all be described as being *wide*.

Further, objects can often be described using more than one measuring word. This book can help a child give as full a description of an object as possible. For instance, a chest of drawers might be described using the Science Buzzwords *heavy*, *large*, *wide*, and *full*.

Some of the pages introduce children to the concept of comparison. This concept can be applied to almost all the Science Buzzwords in the book. A sandwich that is either *thick* or *thin* could be compared with other sandwiches that are even *thicker* or *thinner*.

Once children understand the concept of comparing two objects, they can begin to arrange three or more objects in order by size. For example, a group of children could take pencil and paper and trace around their bare feet. The various drawings could then be arranged by length from the shortest to the longest.

For Further Study —
Activities

1. **People Pictures** — You will need a roll of old wallpaper. Roll out a length of the wallpaper, with the plain side up. Lie down on the paper, and ask a friend to trace around you. Color or paint the outline that has been traced. Cut the outline out, and hang it on a wall or door. Help your friends make outlines of themselves, too, and then compare them to see who is the *tallest*.

2. **Jigsaw Puzzles** — Find two old greeting cards. Cut one card into four *large* pieces. Cut the other card into many *small* pieces. Now try to put the shapes back together to make the pictures whole again. Which puzzle is easier and faster to put back together? Why?

3. **Guessing Game** — Find two small boxes that are exactly the same. Empty, clean ice cream containers would be just right. Fill one box with something *light*, such as cotton balls, and the other with something *heavy*, such as stones. Close the lids, and ask a friend to look at the boxes and guess which one is heavier. Your friend may think that both boxes weigh the same. Now let your friend pick up the boxes. Which is heavier? Try playing this game with many different kinds of objects.

4. **Pet Show** — Make up categories for a pet show using Science Buzzwords from this book. For example, you could have a category for the *tallest* pet or the pet with the *shortest* tail. Then put on a pet show with stuffed animals. Make ribbons out of construction paper for prizes.

5. **Fill 'er Up** — Estimate, or guess, how many glasses of water it will take to fill a plastic pitcher. Then see how close your estimate was by pouring water, glass by glass, into the pitcher. Repeat your experiment with a different size glass.

6. **Balancing Act** — Make a simple balance using common items like a ruler, thick marker or glue stick, and tape. Tape the marker or glue stick on a solid surface, such as a countertop. Then balance the ruler on the marker or glue stick. Use your balance to compare how heavy things are. For example, put a bean on one side and a paper clip on the other. Can you tell which of these is *heavier*?

7. **Tall Tale** — Make up a tall tale, like "Jack and the Beanstalk," using as many Science Buzzwords as possible. For example, your story could be about the *tallest* giant in the land who was unhappy because he lived in the *shortest* house.

8. **Opposite Pairs** — Match up the Science Buzzwords in this book that are opposite pairs, like *wide* and *narrow*. With a friend, try to think of as many other opposite pairs as you can.

Places to Visit

Betty Brinn Children's Museum
929 East Wisconsin Avenue
Milwaukee, WI 53202

Children's Museum
Museum Wharf
300 Congress Street
Boston, MA 02210

Children's Museum of Indianapolis
3000 North Meridian Street
Indianapolis, IN 46206

Discovery Place
301 North Tryon Street
Charlotte, NC 28202

Discovery World
712 West Wells Street
Milwaukee, WI 53233

Exploratorium
3601 Lyon Street
San Francisco, CA 94123

Los Angeles Children's Museum
310 North Main Street
Los Angeles, CA 90012

Museum of Science and Industry
57th Street and Lake Shore Drive
Chicago, IL 60637

Ontario Science Center
770 Don Mills Road
North York, Ontario M3C 1T3

Science Center of British Columbia
1455 Quebec Street
Vancouver, British Columbia V6A 3Z7

Science Museum Of Minnesota
30 East Tenth Street
St. Paul, MN 55101

The Smithsonian Institution
Information Center
1000 Jefferson Drive SW
Washington, D.C. 20560

Books

Balloon Science. Etta Kaner (Addison-Wesley)

Easy Science Experiments. Diane Molleson and Sarah Savage (Scholastic)

Exploring Our Senses (series). Henry Pluckrose (Gareth Stevens)

First Step Science (series). Kay Davies and Wendy Oldfield (Gareth Stevens)

Hands-On Science (series). (Gareth Stevens)

How To Be a Nature Detective. Millicent Selsam (HarperCollins)

The Magic School Bus: Science Explorations. (Scholastic)

Making Shapes. Gary Gibson (Copper Beech Books)

My First Science Book. Angela Wilkes (Knopf)

Science Arts. Mary Ann Kohl and Jean Potter (Bright Ring Publishing)

Science Can Be Fun. Keith Wicks (Lerner Publications)

Web Sites

http://www.waterw.com/~science/kids.html

http://www.islandnet.com/~yesmag/

Videos

Moving A Hippo. (Children's Television International)

My First Science Video. (Sony)

Numbers. (Lucerne Media)

Playing With Air. (Journal Films and Video)

Science. (Agency for Instructional Technology)

Science Rock. (Kimbo Educational)

Seeing Things. (Beacon Films)

Index